CW00455442

Inferences From Haunted Houses And Haunted Men

You are holding a reproduction of an original work that is in the public domain in the United States of America, and possibly other countries.You may freely copy and distribute this work as no entity (individual or corporate) has a copyright on the body of the work.This book may contain prior copyright references, and library stamps (as most of these works were scanned from library copies).These have been scanned and retained as part of the historical artifact.

This book may have occasional imperfections such as missing or blurred pages, poor pictures, errant marks, etc. that were either part of the original artifact, or were introduced by the scanning process. We believe this work is culturally important, and despite the imperfections, have elected to bring it back into print as part of our continuing commitment to the preservation of printed works worldwide. We appreciate your understanding of the imperfections in the preservation process, and hope you enjoy this valuable book.

INFERENCES
FROM HAUNTED HOUSES
AND HAUNTED MEN

Copyright secured in U.S.A.

INFERENCES
ROM HAUNTED HOUSES
AND HAUNTED MEN

BY THE

HONBLE. JOHN HARRIS

PHILIP WELLBY

6 HENRIETTA STREET, COVENT GARDEN

LONDON

1901

Phil 7060.48

B ✱

HARVARD COLLEGE LIBRARY
FROM THE
PHILOSOPHICAL LIBRARY
OF
WILLIAM JAMES
1923

Inferences from Haunted Houses
and Haunted Men

THE lack of interest in so-called psychical matters is somewhat surprising.

There is, however, more hope of the clearing up of the scientific aspects of these phenomena than ever before.

Sir William Crookes, late President of the British Association, has no doubt that thoughts and images may be transferred from one mind to another without the agency of the recognised organs of sense, and that knowledge may enter the human mind without being communicated in any hitherto known or recognised ways! The word recognised is important; perhaps "not by the recognised action of the organs of sense," would be a better expression.

In the "Alleged Haunting of B—— House," p. 33, Miss Freer says: "Apparitions are really hallucinations or false impressions upon the senses, created so far as originated by any external cause, by other minds either in the body or out of the body, which are themselves invisible in the ordinary and physical sense of the term, and really acting through some means at present very imperfectly known." This would include hypnotism at a distance, but also perhaps spirits.

Dr. Gowers has recently (reported in the *Lancet*), in a speech at University College, pointed out the close connection of the optic and auditory nerves with regard to cases of deafness.

The young lady who, when an attempt at transferring the sight of a candle to her was made, heard the word candle or something like it, the first letter doubtful, shows that thought transfer is to the ear as well as to the eye, or at least goes over from one to the other; she says, "You know I as often hear the name of the object as see the thing itself." This may have been from a mental effort to receive distinctly an inefficiently acute impression of her friend's. She saw a *jug* seen by her friend, and heard the train she heard. The colour of the jug differed a little. The distance fourteen *miles.* Audible speech might thus be helped by despatching a picture of the idea from a distance. Other people must be like Miss Campbell.[1] There must be material force in this, since a thought heightens the temperature of the brain. But this force has its limits of distance, &c.

To connect apparitions with hypnotism.

[1] Podmores "Studies," p. 228.

In their case, and in so-called spiritual experiences (spiritistic is the better word), there is generally a preceding feeling like entering an icehouse.[1] This is described as occurring to the butler of the Haunted House at B——, Harold Sanders, in 1896; to Mr. "Endell," and to others. This chill is surely identical with, or very closely related to, the chill of hypnotism mentioned by Binet and Féré.[2] The balance of the circulation has been interfered with. They state that this is the only symptom by which any one can tell he has been hypnotised, and that this is not always present.

In continuous slight hypnotism, chills on part of the scalp, part of the shoulder, part of the face, or the ribs, &c., may be experienced; they are possibly signs of slackening hypnotic power.

[1] "Alleged Haunting," &c., pp. 50, 139.
[2] "Animal Magnetism," chap. xiv.

There is another symptom, hyperæsthesia of the eye, which Binet and Féré
omit; this is extremely rare among men,
and with women results from local affection. The symptom probably appears in
hypnotic cases from the cutaneous lesser
sciatic nerve, which is connected with
the nerves of the sexual system, being
affected.

The chill and the hyperæsthesia of
the eyes can be so severe that a doctor
or an oculist would be consulted.

The feeling of gravel in the eye is
probably produced by light falling through
chinks on the eye when hyperæsthetic
during sleep—the lids may be slightly
tightened, as it were; this is perhaps a
nearer approach to a profounder hypnotism.

"During actual hypnosis," says Mr.
Harry Vincent, "frequently the contrac-
tion of the muscles is so obvious that the

subject appears to be indulging in a grim smile." [1]

I venture to call attention to the grim smile worn by Charles Kingsley in the portrait which prefaces the large edition of his Life and Letters. Charles Kingsley suffered from frequent fits of exhaustion; these are often the results of excessive hypnotism after the limit (at the fifth or sixth effort) of the hypnotist's power has been reached. His brother Henry, we learn from Mr. Kegan Paul's "Memoirs," was excessively hypnotisable. His character was weaker perhaps than Charles's, but the geniality of his writings bears testimony to his remarkable ability.

He was only rescued from a condition little better than a tramp's by a kind friend. Charles's life was perhaps shortened by hypnotism. One of Kingsley's neighbours at Eversley was the late Sir W. Cope.

[1] "Elements of Hypnotism," p. 99.

The elder son of this gentleman, when Secretary of Legation at Stockholm, came to a tragic end. He suddenly, when out walking with a friend, although his health had been apparently perfect, began to shout and wave his umbrella. He was put under the care of attendants, as he was considered to be temporarily insane. He jumped out of a window and was killed. Voices insulting or threatening him, and with such scoundrels speech would be of something dreadful, would provoke or frighten the unhappy man.

About two years later a distinguished priest, well known in London, also suddenly waved an umbrella and behaved as if he were angry. But he showed hardly any sign of insanity, and on applying to the proper court for release from supervision, was declared sane by a jury.

Strength of mind and religious feeling doubtless saved him from the fate of Mr.

Cope. A brave man can resist such an attack under favourable circumstances.

It is well known to those who have read the Biography of Lawrence Oliphant, and that of Dr. Anna Kingsford by Professor Maitland, that Lawrence Oliphant, who became a Shaker (a member of a sect who employ hypnotism, as Mr. H. Vincent describes, to bind their neophytes to them),[1] wrote commonplace vulgar verse on religious subjects, although himself a highly cultivated literary man.

Hypnotism doubtless led to this; the verse thought out in some vulgar Shaker's mind was transferred to Oliphant. Not only was Oliphant induced to become a Shaker, but his wife became one also, and both sacrificed much money to the society and agreed to live in celibacy. Let us continue again from the known to the unknown. Mrs. Lawrence Oliphant's

[1] "Elements of Hypnotism," Appendix, *note* 3, p. 270.

brother, the late Captain Lestrange, R.N., left his ship without leave, to avoid his wife. He had married an undesirable person, who has also been dead some years.

He was a most intelligent officer, and commanded the despatch vessel of the Admiral in command of the Mediterranean fleet. It is most probable that he was weakened by hypnotism, otherwise he would not have entered into this marriage, or allowed himself to be broken down by disgust at its consequences. An exceedingly manly, robust character, and devoted to his profession, he could not without being hypnotised have deserted his ship. The only reason he had for leaving it was that his wife threatened to come to the Mediterranean to Malta. There was a gang of criminal hypnotists on the Mediterranean coast then. Captain Lestrange fled to Copenhagen, a place connected with most of the attacks of criminal hypnotists, mentioned before and hereafter. He had visited it on duty two or three times, and been in contact with others who suffered. He died two or three years afterwards, probably of a broken heart. Here, for the second time, a connection between two victims is traceable.

In the former case, the two were simply neighbours; the probability that in each pair of cases one gang was concerned is very great. One gang, if not both, were connected with Copenhagen; indeed, they may have been the same gang.

If striking haunted house stories are rare, the reason is that, on obvious grounds, gangs of hypnotists are rare also.

The writer believes that Lord Howe's and his sister's courage prompted the attack on them by a gang of hypnotists 120 years ago.[1] Poltergeist disturbances

---

[1] A. Lang's "Ghost Stories."

are caused by a single person generally;
it is not impossible that in rare cases
there is a confederate.

These victims of hypnotists were thus
four—two very eminent literary men, distinguished also in other ways; a very
rising naval officer; and a diplomatist, a
member of the foremost of the services
of the Crown.

Father B. was attacked in 1888–89 in
London. In June 1892, Father H. visited
the Haunted House at B——. He first
brought the haunting to the notice of
Lord Bute in August 1892, and in 1893
met a lady who had been governess at
B—— about twelve years before, and
who reported that the house was haunted
then.

A noise like the continual explosion of
petards, another like the falling of a large
animal against his bedroom door, another
noise like spirit raps, and shrieks were

heard by Father H.; no one else then heard them. Father H. heard them for eight nights, and not on the ninth. . As a priest, he was probably a good deal alone, and had to walk over to a cottage behind a belt of wood to the eastward, where the retreat of the nuns he attended to was held.

According to the average experience of Miss Freer's party, he would only have been attacked on about two days. The last day his tormentor left—doubtless to avoid a journey with Father H. and sub-sequent recognition. How these sounds are produced is easily understood. If the doctrine of a very light stream of elec-tricity be admitted, the pressure on the ear readily causes raps—there is a slight buzzing sound if the pressure on the ear be relaxed at a distance at first, later there is pain; the flap is from an inter-mitted pressure. It is a thud if the pressure be more acute, and the pattering, which is almost identical to the effect produced by a drop of water rolling on the inside of a sensitive ear, occurs when there is a double or treble intermission. In some cases where the victim is strong, the consonants can be worked off to his hearing.

Add to this a slight effect on the eye, and Miss Campbell's doubtfully pronounced word "candle" becomes clear enough. An initial starts a word there is some reason to believe. Mr. Osgood Mason dwells upon community of sensation, and it is doubtless this that renders the direction of aim so exact; but when the subject of tickled faces is considered, we shall see that it does not insure complete accuracy, any more than that exists in volley firing, which with inferior shots is more telling than independent firing, and yet is not perfect.

The reason why more audile phenomena are perceived at night is that the
percipient is tolerably still. Father H.
and other people heard these sounds more
when in bed after daylight. If loud
clangs, &c., were heard by night by the
garrison under Miss Freer's command, it
was that the attacking hypnotists did not
have the chances they had with Father
H. of hypnotising their victims; and here
again, where action on the ear and eye
is concerned, talking with a friend, or
indeed any one, is a great safeguard.
The tympanum is stirred, the eye moves
—the mere irregularity of the breath is
an aid. Another reason will be given
later. Miss Campbell, whose case—one
of experimental thought transference—has
been twice referred to, was an intimate
friend of Miss Despard, who effected the
transfers. Her case differs from his; he
expected nothing (at least consciously),

and perceived nothing except ugly sounds, until he got a feeling that some one was glad that he left, and that he himself would not like to pass another night there. Perhaps this last feeling was a deceptive transfer; they did not like the stout priest bluffing them. Later he was willing to go to the house at B——— again.

Miss Campbell got a word, imperfect perhaps, but a better-developed effort developed better results. It is worth remarking that in another experimental transfer of thought, where the percipient was not warned, when Mr. Godfrey's apparition was seen by a lady friend, she heard a curious sound like birds in the ry. It is by no means unlikely that his was the result of his first trying to attract her attention.[1]

The eye impression moving to the ear

[1] Podmore's " Studies," p. 250.

in a new and strange way, there is perhaps a stirring and dragging of the cartilages.

That Mr. Godfrey's friend appeared in response and spoke to him, and referred back to some joint conversation, is curious.

It must be said here that the speech coming from within is extremely indicative of a real transferred or hypnotic speech, and its coming from within facilitates surprise where it is used fraudulently or criminally. A certain amount of collateral trickery would enhance this. It is easily confounded with the victim's own thoughts.

The appearance of a person to another does not seem to be as difficult as the causing another person to appear to a third person. In this case the second person should apparently be hypnotised, and willed to appear to the third. The third person must know the second person.[1]

The apparition to Miss Ducane is interesting, and it is a pity it could not be recognised.[2]   It was seen in the mirror by her sisters, with one exception; but she (Miss Ducane) and the other young ladies all felt the cold air.

Miss Freer, who saw the shadows of a figure on the wall first, and then the figure itself, must have been more scientifically operated on, but an apparition to several young ladies is harder to bring about.   The original of Miss Freer's visions should be carefully traced — the one in the drawing-room especially. How many persons would be needed to produce the rather inchoate phenomena observed by Miss Freer's garrison is doubtful; three distinct voices, if not four, were

[1] Osgood Mason, " Telepathy," &c., chap. x.
[2] Podmore's " Studies," p. 275.

B

heard,[1] and it seems probable that at least four persons would be necessary to produce very startling phenomenon—notably conversation.[2]

All the ears and eyes (notably one eye, the right) are affected. This number would be easily got from a body like the Shakers, but it is probably harder to collect an efficient gang elsewhere. Indeed there is, the writer believes, evidence that only one such gang exists, and its members are possibly all British subjects of various colours. It is strange there have been no informers. The failure of the minor gang at B—— to fairly beat Miss Freer's party as they had beaten the family who lived in the house the year before, made them furious, and their attacks on the weak secular priests and on a French lady of high courage but

---

[1] "Alleged Haunting of B—— House," p. 134.
[2] "Haunting of B—— House," p. 121.

weak health, were particularly desperate.
How far the latter's health was under-
mined, and her death brought about by
them, is uncertain. She had the shock
of the fire at the Paris charity bazaar to
break her down. She lost relations there.
Miss Freer sometimes writes as if ghosts
and spirits were possible. In her essays,
on page 52, she says "naughty girls or
spirits"—the collation is perhaps sufficient
to condemn the latter alternative. But
her remark about a lady medium whom
she compares to a gentleman jockey, and
who had a maid of the Catholic faith,
and that this fact had an effect on the
later proceedings, reads as if she were
not wanting in scepticism. Probably Miss
Freer, subject to thought transference,
and yet a thought transferrer, as she
is, was interested in the effect on Miss
" K." of the Catholic maid-servant. Nothing more interesting than the transfer

of thought by Miss Freer to a friend, who therefore saw candles lighted on a lunch table, could be found, but here again the experience seems simply hypnotic. The chapters in her essays on visual- ising,[1] on "how it once came into my head," are very valuable. Those on hauntings are grave and gay, comments on realities and errors and superstitious, sometimes charming, beliefs. Miss Freer says of the visions which she sees of persons in the crystal, or otherwise, that they are (1) visions of the living—clair- voyant or telepathic; (2) visions of the departed, having no obvious relation to time and space; (3) visions which are more or less of the nature of pictures, from memory or imagination: they are like No. 2, but not of a person.

Her most remarkable stories are cer- tainly almost magical. One refers to her

[1] A. Goodrich Freer's "Essays," p. 126.

seeing the doings of relations, another to
her seeing a friend's doings.[1] " The figures
do not appear" (she says, referring to
the B—— apparitions) " before 6.30 at
the earliest ; there is little light on their
surfaces—they show by their own light—
i.e. outlined by a thread of light."[2]

She does not see things in a flash.
Thus when she saw a brown wood crucifix,
she saw a hand holding it, whilst a clergy-
man who saw the same crucifix (Father
H. also saw it) got just a glimpse of it.
It was also seen by Miss Langton.[3]

To turn to another characteristic of the
disturbers of the peace at B——, and to
illustrate it by comparison. In Mr. Podmore's book on Psychical research,[4] in
the chapter describing phenomena of the
Poltergeist order—the Poltergeist in one

---

[1] " Haunting of B—— House," p. 102.
[2] *Ibid.*, p. 142. [3] *Ibid.*, p. 132.
[4] " Studies," p. 153.

case was a girl of about twelve, Alice. She, Mrs. B. and Miss B., and Miss K. were seated at a table; it moved sharply and struck Miss K. on the arm. Miss K. was an inmate of the house, and no doubt Alice preferred hitting her to hitting her mother and sister.

Similarly the disturbers at B—— House showed great respect for the press. When a leading Edinburgh editor's son was there all was quiet; and although they flew at their pet prey the priests, yet a bishop was too imposing for them; and after he had blessed the house from top to bottom, they left it quiet for the remaining week of Miss Freer's stay.[1]

This might be sufficient to lull any further zeal the Catholic regular clergy might find for the matter.

Again the strange fact may be noted that, a gardener coming every night to

[1] "Alleged Haunting," p. 215.

look after the stoves between 10 and 10.30, no noises were noted at that time, with one exception.   The gardener therefore kept the ghosts away.

But the one exception was when a servants' ball was being given, and the gardener was in the house, in the billiard-room, where the supper was served.   To obtain re-hypnotism it was necessary for the disturbers to approach the house. Their object would easily be affected with people already hypnotised in the railway station or train.

These would suffer from fatigue and nervousness, but would put it down to the journey.

The approach to the house with rights of way close by would be very easy. The brave garrison who were so well commanded by Miss Freer, and who, with three or four exceptions, support her account, were generally affected (if well known, and not as Mr. Z., the editor's son, too dangerous) on the first night of their arrival at B——.

Miss Freer and Miss Moore, her comrade who shared her bedroom during the greater part of the B—— siege, were thus attacked. Mr. L. F. was disturbed, and also Colonel Taylor (in whose name the house was taken, and who was almost impervious to influences), on their first night at B——. Why the Honourable E. F. did not suffer at all is not clear. Perhaps he was left alone on account of his scientific capacities.

Three gentlemen who arrived together were not affected; there is strength in numbers; and whilst people talking to each other are harder to influence for two or three reasons, they further unconsciously watch over each other. Mr. W. stayed two days and heard nothing; his scepticism was convinced later. Mr. MacP.

experienced nothing in four nights, but on a later visit heard sounds. Mr. C., an Edinburgh solicitor, heard voices in the glen, on the second occasion of a vision being seen there by Miss Freer, which was during his first visit.

Perhaps it may be guessed that the three gentlemen travelled with no heavy luggage, and their identity and destination was not detected. The vision seen most was that of a nun in the black dress commonest among nuns.

It was seen moving about on a very steep bank, a bank apparently too steep for walking, and was only visible against the snow. Miss Freer did not look on the bank for tracks.

It may be noted that on the two previous days in the neighbourhood of this glen a terrier, who never barked except under strong excitement, had barked at the same hour, but no vision was seen ; on the 6th of February the dog had been taken off in another direction. After seeing the vision in the glen, Miss Freer almost always heard strange sounds at night.

The inference is that in the glen, where there was plenty of cover, and where, judging by the dog's barking, suspicious persons lurked, Miss Freer was hypnotised, made to see an apparition, and left susceptible to a further operation that night. Later on it says, " the dog ran up, pointed, and ran straight for the two women." This was on the second occasion of a grey woman appearing, and the third occasion of the black nun being seen. He was found barking in the glen ; no cause could be found; a lurking stranger is a possible explanation. It may be noted, that the pointing attitude in a dog of the smaller breeds means reflection, and that something puzzled it, perhaps its mistress's attitude; but its going on barking would indicate the steady retreat of some one who frightened it.

At least three voices were heard—perhaps more. Phenomena were scarce; the gang's powers were still limited, though the horror they inflicted showed that they reached the bounds of some of the victims' strength. Miss Freer not only heard sounds in the house, where she was less exposed than in the glen, but saw apparitions on four occasions.

The visions that can be inflicted telepathically, *i.e.* hypnotically, seem to be at first limited to two kinds—first, the vision of the person himself: this hallucination has often been effected by honest experimentalists; secondly, and this is rather matter of inference, a rascal who has hypnotised a person may be unable to get rid of the image of his victim, and transfers the ghost that haunts him to another subject.

The portrait of a so-called Nathan Early, at the beginning of Osgood Mason's book, has the eyebrows, eyes, and mouth of a much mesmerised man. The mouth has not become stiffened into a laugh, as he was of a gentle firm disposition, and the hypnotism probably was from a distance.

The possessed hypnotist transferred it to his victim, Mrs. Juliette Burton.

The qualification, "at first," is important; visions are perhaps not easily transferred to a new subject, but the question of what is good policy for the rascals may have to be considered. This may limit the experience of those who have been more seriously victimised than Miss Freer and her garrison were.

The experiments reported in Mr. Podmore's excellent book, though invaluable, are probably not exhaustive.

Colonel Meysey Thompson's Remi-
niscences relate a wonderful occurrence
connected with his father, but it is
believed that more striking matters oc-
curred even than this.   To return to the
haunted house.

The cottage to the east of the glen—
Ballechin cottage—(there is no reason for
not using the name except that B—— is
shorter than Ballechin ; indeed the public
and the Perthshire police should combine
to clear the neighbourhood of the gang
who have troubled a charming country
house)—was once a place for retreat for
nuns.   The fact was not known to Miss
Freer and her friends until several visions
of nuns had been seen in the glen.[1]

The poor religious women, like the
priests, must have been a favourite prey
of the hypnotists.

The   writer   believes   that   the   late

[1] " Haunting of B—— House," p. 136.

Cardinal Manning approved of religious ladies residing with their families and carrying on works of charity, a less wretched life than the usual nun's life often unavoidably must be. English Catholics have not been subjected to the terrors of a *casa de exercitios* such as broke the courage of Mrs. Grahame's spinster friend.[1] It must have been extremely repulsive to the feelings of a m anlike Bishop Guerrero, and doubtless did not continue to exist long even in remote Chile.

But subdued in spirit as they are, the attacks of hypnotists would be terribly felt by most nuns.

Father H.'s apparition was seen by Miss Langton in a dream or vision. She recognised him when she met him three months later; he may have been shadowed by some of the hypnotists for

[1] Grahame's " Chile."

purposes of information ; and the idea
that he should be begged to aid in
blessing the house and banning the
haunters, may have been a thought
transferred by a hypnotist to Miss
Freer, who is liable to thought transfer,
and is a good transferrer herself. Why
should not a nun's apparition be transferred as was Father H.'s (to Miss
Langton) ?

It appears that valiant resistance can
inflict this possession upon hypnotists as
well as the horrors of a hard and disgust-
ing victory do.

Perhaps the Scin-laeca of Bulwer's
" Harold," the apparition of Cerdic,
haunted the imaginations of generations
of magicians. These were possibly Celts ;
only one witch-rune on a Saxon sword
was found ; that was in the Isle of Wight.
It was, Professor Stephens said, a soli-
tary instance, as the brave Germans

thought magic the art of a coward. The hypnotism from which all the garrison suffered was a slight hypnotism; the eyes remained open and people went about behaving almost normally. Father B. lost his self-control for an instant. Some people would have to be tricked in a complicated way. Thought transfer—audible to the person affected alone, or even inaudible but perceptible like a thought—accounts for the whole of Mrs. Piper's operations; she might have accomplices who would never be seen speaking to her, and who would dictate actions, say, to one of the Pelham or Howard family. These dictated actions, or inchoate plans, would then be reported by Mrs. Piper writing as George Pelham. What Mrs. Piper saw or felt or heard would be—at least at stated times—seen or felt or heard by her fellow conspirators. As in conjuring everything found was placed beforehand in the desired position. Thus facts recounted had been induced. The blackguard who spoke to her as Phinuit was less educated than the one who dictated George Pelham's communications.

Mrs. Piper's education was rather suited to receive the vulgar Phinuit's, than the more refined pseudo Pelham's communications. But the progress from the one stage so revolting to Miss Freer, to the other so delightful, a sign of increased refinement to Mr. Myers, was hardly more a change than the turning on a hot tap after a cold water tap into a basin. The receptacle was the same. But as a strong hypnotist herself, Mrs. Piper could bring off the Sutton matter; she could easily give Mrs. Sutton visual hallucinations. The startling position taken up by Mr. Myers in his article in the *National Review*, is easily ex-

C

plicable. He and Dr. Hodgson were magnetised by Mrs. Piper, and were like wax in her hands. Eusapia Palladius has the same power.

It is a sad declension in an eminent classic, that he, whose reference to the primitive heathen Ulysses torturing the shade of his own mother is rather revolting than elevating, should be full of wonder and delight at it.

After all Ulysses was the worthy ancestor of many a pirate hanged at Malta, more ferocious enemies of man than the Red Indian. Some somnambulists should be perhaps protected from exploitation. Mrs. Piper's trance is presumably feigned, as trances can easily be.

To return to Haunted Houses. In a haunted house case, a story suggested by some chronological connection, or the nature of the apparition, is attached to the phenomena. No doubt, in these days where the individuals who perceive the phenomena have a wider experience, such a variety of persons appear that the ghostly appearance loses its individuality if not its authenticity.   Mr. Podmore discusses such cases.[1]   In Mr. Podmore's book when Poltergeists, Cock-lore ghost affairs, are discussed, it appears that genuine hallucinations may be associated with fraudulent physical phenomena.

These are, it may be positively stated, hypnotic hallucinations.   The two together in some cases, as in the one already mentioned[2] of "Alice," amount to a very good ghost story, the blood on the floor alone excepted.   Alice's home was a terrace house in a town.   The House at B—— was very large and somewhat lonely.

It is, however, less than 200 yards

---

[1] "Studies," pp. 305–308 ; Chap. x. Haunted Houses.
[2] "Podmore," p. 153.

from a road along the Tay, that river running parallel to its front to the southward of it.

Rights of way from the north-west pass north of the house, and there were some empty lodges there; these might afford shelter to the persons of strong hypnotic power who chose to play the ghost. The continuity of the noises at night would be thus facilitated. The house belonged to the grand-nephew of a retired Indian major. It is apparently suggested that the major's relations with a young housekeeper were suspicious. The two and a native Indian servant are buried in the kirkyard at L——; presumably Logierait.

The haunted house is, as was said, at Ballechin in Perthshire; and it may be noted that to Perthshire Esdaile, the famous Calcutta hypnotist and physician, retired; but that he was unable to effect

with the Perthshire people the marvellous
cures he had brought about in India.
Perhaps the Indian servant may have
attracted the attention of some base
imitator of the honourable Esdaile. It
may be noted that an officer of rank,
whose family were friends and not very
distant neighbours in the south of England
of the late Rev. Lord Sydney Godolphin
Osborne, experienced some singular phenomena. Lord Sydney was a great
hypnotist, and cured, or believed he cured,
many cases of epilepsy. The officer in
question suffered at times from a tickling
in his face, which annoyed him very
much ; it seemed to be more on the cheeks
than in the corners behind the nostrils.

The connection with hypnotism is seen
in the next case. A much younger man,
a captain in the Indian army, who had
attended many spiritist seances, suffered
much the same sort of tickling annoyance.

Both were perfectly sane, and were doubtless persecuted. They were intelligent,
capable people. A friend informs the
writer that when some years ago he
visited a fortune-teller of the Mrs. Piper
class in London, he had a cold trickling
up his feet, doubtless from hypnotism,
to help thought reading.

The tickling of the face is the result
of a more or less vain attempt to reach
the ear or eye. It will be felt by people
driving whose ear and eye would otherwise be affected. People sleeping in an
exposed place may suffer more, as the
fixed recumbent position makes them ob-
noxious to attack, as was previously remarked. The hyperæsthesia spreads in a
slight degree round the eye.

The nature of the eye is hardly
understood yet; it is quite possible that
subconscious pictures pass before us like
a cinematograph, enforcing or enforced

by our thoughts. It has been remarked that thought is a species of self-hypnotism. Hypnotism may only make these pictures more distinct and modify them by degrees. In the attempt to inflict a picture on the eye, only the dark image of it may be seen. The writer believes that this means failure to affect the mind. Binet and Féré mention the dark after-shadow.

The extremest direct effect of hypnotism upon the eye, mechanically speaking, is doubtless scarcely more than the shock of thistledown wafted against it by a gentle breeze. It appears to affect the corners of the eye; the electric film is perhaps divided by the approach over the skin to another and damper tissue. But hyperæsthesia sometimes spreads to the upper cheek.

Madame de Maceine saw Rubinstein's hallucinatory picture with the corner of

her eye.[1] A shock even as slight as
a bit of thistledown blown against the
cornea might be ill-timed at a street-
crossing. Mr. S. of B—— was run over
in the streets of London and killed. He
had been previously hypnotically affected,
for he heard quantities of raps; these
were no friendly signs of spirits, but the
affection of his early hypnotists practising
against him.

A double image is seen, the eye being
curiously affected, when for instance the
knobs of a chest of drawers appeared
through the apparition.

The vision is in the veil or mist of Ibn
Khaldoon. Does not this cast a light
upon the conceptive and receptive powers
of the eye. The conceptive power is
shown, as Binet and Féré remark, by
the fact that our imagination has done
away with the end of a nerve which

[1] *Vide* a leading article, *Daily News*, July 23.

should be seen at every instant of our
lives.   Light images may be given by
feeble hypnotists of which but the dark
reaction can be detected only once in a
way.   Compare Binet and Féré.   They
are perhaps noted when hypnotic speech
does not come off and is not heard.
The small vision in one eye only is
separate from the landscape, and practi-
cally does not much influence the mind
of the person on whom it is inflicted,
who continues aware that it is a mere
delusion, causing scarcely anything but
trifling interruption.   This is perhaps only
the case with the few, more numerous
however amongst the strong nations than
amongst the weaker ones, who are impervious to ordinary hypnotism, or could
only be hypnotised if extraordinarily
fatigued.

The development of intelligence and
perhaps endurance increases the number

of these. I imagine the students in Germany, whom Heidenhain found so superior to our British students, were not only better educated, as is usual, but were also fighting club men, hardened to pain, and very superior to the bulk of their British contemporaries in courage and endurance.

The word skin-deep hypnotism might well be applied to the cases just mentioned. To show instances of its criminal use. Hypnotism has been used, there is reason to believe, against an Austrian ambassador in Petersburg, who found his papers in disorder, and saw a pale young man in his study. Ordering the gates to be closed, he was told by the porter that no one had entered, but that the ghost of the son of a former ambassador—a lad the writer knew who died at the Embassy —haunted the house. The ghost was therefore a hallucination inflicted on the ambassador. Stepniak's death at a level-crossing on a railway, might be brought about as Mr. Stewart's was in the street. Prince Alexander of Battenburg's mental prostration might be brought about by the same means when he was kidnapped.

At the time of the dispute between England and Russia, caused by Penjdeh, a Greek naval officer showed a slightly indiscreet attachment for England. Shortly afterwards he was removed for a time from the post he held, as he was considered not quite sane ; he had been at Copenhagen, He was, however, restored to the navy, as it was considered rather good for his health than otherwise that he should go to sea. He and an English diplomatist at Copenhagen had been at Fiume together on duty, and the former was undoubtedly tricked by hypnotists, pretending to be acting for freemasonry, a trick played since on another person, and before in England on a third. It has also been played in Italy long ago. The voices would be taken for ventriloquists, whilst scenes heard would be considered to be perceived in catalepsy by a person in good health, and in full possession of his faculties, if not a doctor. At Fiume is the Whitehead torpedo manufactory, but as the hammering and other noises connected with it would prevent the chief persons in charge of the factory from being got at, the hypnotists were doubtless foiled there. Of course they may have got some information indirectly, but nothing of high value.

The alarm produced at B—— House was brought about less by the phenomena than by the pressure on the vagus nerve or heart. Whether fatal syncope can be produced by modifying the heart beats, as Mr. Vincent suggests it can, is of course a question for a doctor. He seems to think such cases not uncommon. A gentleman attacked by hypnotists twice suffered from syncope. He was previously suffering from exhaustion brought on by rowing a party for their lives in a squall, and took strychnine at a doctor's orders; that medicament, as is known, makes the nerves more sensitive. Further rascally attempts were a failure in better-situated houses. The terror of hearing a voice suddenly is in those circumstances very great; against one in good health it is less, no doubt. The trouble given at B—— was particularly great in the case of Miss Moore,[1] who scarcely slept for a week; she was Miss Freer's comrade in No. 1, the S.W. corner room of the house at B——, and the most exposed room where voices were chiefly heard; and that, too, by almost every one who slept there, Miss N., the Rev. Mr. Q., Father MacL.,

---

[1] "Alleged Haunting of B—— House," p. 118.

and Madame Boisseaux. The road ran nearest to it there. The writer believes that the remarkable fact that No. 1, the S.W. room, No. 2, the W. room, No. 3, the N.W. room, showed a far higher average of phenomena than the other five—*i.e.* the three eastern and the north and south centre rooms — is accounted for by the following circumstances.

No. 8, the south room, was much exposed, but unlike No. 1, it had no door in a line with another door and a window. Upon No. 1 an almost direct attack could be made from northward or southward; for the partition walls of the house, as well as the outer walls, were very thick.[1]

In the new part of the house these were less so, but people in them were less affected than had been the case when the H. family stayed there.

[1] "Alleged Haunting of B—— House," p. 94; *ibid.*, p. 140, *note.*

Rooms Nos. 1, 2, and 3 could be raked
from north or south.   Nearly all the
persons in the house were affected, and
leaving out one or two men who objected
to being reported, it appears that the
ladies, who spent in the aggregate 237
nights in the house, had sixty-two noc-
turnal experiences, whilst men spending
108 nights had twenty experiences (between bedtime and breakfast was considered night-time).   But three of the
eleven ladies were very sensitive; only
one man out of fourteen was so.   Therefore, on a fair estimate, men and women
were about equally sensitive; and this
is the case with hypnotism generally.
A further proof of the nature of the
attack.

With regard to rooms Nos. 1 and 2, the
following curious fact is noted by Miss
Langton.   "The knocks on the door
between Nos. 1 and 2 have been audible

in this room; No. 2 in my experience only when No. 2 is empty; and in No. 1 only when No. 2 is empty."[1] This looks as if attacks were made from the opposite side of the house to make detection less easy, especially by daylight. The maid-servants in the attics were often more impressed than the people in the rooms below. This seems due to the construction of the house; the attics are more approachable than the rooms from the staircase. The electricity follows the track of a person far better on a stair than on a ladder, it may be remarked. Thick walls, high window - sills, a commanding position, and a murmuring brook, are great securities against hypnotism, and these would be found in older Scotch castles. Another element of safety, the purling brook, is here mentioned; all noise

[1] "Alleged Haunting of B—— House," p. 169.

is a good antidote; it is perhaps the case that with hypnotism from a distance the hypnotic state is continually waxing and waning, one link, generally a weaker one, succeeding another in the chain of impressions on the temperament. The diminution being continual, the force is renewed by people getting near enough to get a strong hold again, otherwise it dies out.

These approaches were doubtless most dangerous on railway journeys; hypnotism acts better in a small room than in a large one, and therefore a person in a railway carriage is more affected. Here discomfort and oppression helps hypnotism, but the hypnotist if in the train is in a favourable position, as the distance is preserved very closely and need not be very great.

Carriages are of the same size, and this is doubtless a help to the operator. The

D

frequency of phenomena being observed on the night of arrival has been noticed. Miss N., who drove over, was not affected. The average recurrence of phenomena to each person was every fourth night; other people besides those previously mentioned as suffering on first nights, were on the second visit Miss Langton and Miss Duff. The latter was only very restless. This resembles the experimental result obtained by Mr. Rose; he attempted to impress two ladies in the same house: the elder saw his apparition, the younger was only restless.[1]

It may be noted that in intercourse with other people, some effort is commonly made to secure their attention; this no doubt is connected with the greater facility for causing one's own apparition to be presented.

Thus to resume the question of place

---

[1] "Podmore," p. 252.

of hypnotism, on the second sojourn four
people suffered in the night of first arrival.
Was the gang larger, or were the assailants operators who had been afraid of the
cold before?

Possibly Miss Langton had been
followed to St. Andrews, where she had
spent Easter, and had a vision of the
phantom nun. In other cases where the
absence had been longer only two people
were attacked.

Several other persons felt a restlessness
like Miss Duff's—woke without any cause,
&c.—Mrs. M., Mr. T., Mr. L. F., and
others. If any doubt be felt about the
appearances and noises being from hypnotism, the experimental cases should re-
move it, the resemblance of the feelings
of the "garrison" to those hypnotised
should be dwelt on, the times of recurrence, and finally later mentioned the
peculiarity of the apparition's nature—

corresponding to those produced by hypnotism. The argument that Féré and Binet are fond of, that hypnotism much resembles what can be seen every day, is no doubt true.

Mrs. Anna Kingsford appears to have been often hypnotised by some unknown rascal, but her gentle admirable character seems to have suffered but little, though her life was possibly shortened.

But when Professor Maitland talks of building walls round her, he emphasises the advantage that society gives against witchcraft. Of four people whose lives have been destroyed or grievously injured by hypnotism, whose circumstances are known to the writer, three were childless married men (two were unhappily married), and the fourth case was a bachelor's, a poor young man's.

It may be noted that in the North of Europe, at least half a small class of men were attacked, and the others were more or less connected with these. The most were diplomatists and consuls.

The advantage of society must be referred to a great extent to the stream of thought-transfer from hypnotists being checked and broken up; for the effect of this stream being made indirect or semi-direct, its dominating power is thereby greatly diminished.

On the other hand, in three cases where attacks were defeated, the subjects were happily married men, and in two, if not in the three (the third case the writer gathered at second hand and fortunately remembered later), they had children. On the third visit of Miss Freer to B—— that lady notes that "the influence is evil and horrible. The worn features at breakfast were really a dismal sight."[1]

On this occasion it looks as if more

[1] "Haunting of B—— House," p. 210.

than three persons (Miss Langton on the 19th of February had noted three voices) were engaged in the attack.

The writer has no doubt, from personal and observed experience, that sometimes transfer is used, but is doubtful to what extent.

Boxes on the ear, slaps on the back, nay a flip as with a towel on the bare back, are felt, the last even by a clothed person. In Poltergeist cases, as in Alice's, a slap on the back was felt; perhaps she hypnotised Miss K. and slapped her on the back and transferred the slap to her (Alice's) mother.

This would be like the two engineer students' case, where the hypnotised one appeared to a friend.

In Poltergeist cases, one person perhaps does the mischief; in inferior haunted house cases two would be enough. The Poltergeist raisers are often subject to fits ; the people who are vicious attackers, like the assailants of the occupants of B——, must be semi-maniacs. The terror is sometimes brought about by two people operating ; one producing a terrifying effect, the other intensifying the terror. In attempting to weaken a person to whom speech has been made intelligible at a distance, a sensation would be transferred after the speech, so that he might believe it affected him, and cease jeering at and despising the operator. A man with some knowledge of mesmerism, and living a life with good interests in it, could defy them : such a case has happened. For nearly fifty years a gentleman was tormented at times, and died and lived sane.

The attack has perhaps been more developed in the last twenty or thirty years, the influence of above-board hypnotism acted upon that practised by criminal scoundrels. A combination possible is, for instance, one rascal showing a faint image of a fiend, and another transmitting a sound like a scratching at a window; this was a failure, the percipient believing that the devil acted under the authority of the Almighty, and had no business with innocent people. It was given to a person in a semi-sleeping condition. Pain combined was efficient. The pain is partly by affection of cutaneous nerves — partly by affection of the ear; but no one on the watch would be driven into lunatic acts by it. Of course after exhaustion (and pain makes this easier) the victim may be in a stupefied condition and obey: this is the post-hypnotic state, which will not come off with people who have been instructed against this villainous game. Miss Freer's admirable nerve was doubtless due to the habit of studying phenomena. The worn features at breakfast, mentioned before, included those of two secular priests. Miss Freer had failed to get permission for three well - known priests belonging to societies (perhaps Jesuits) to come. The gentleman already mentioned who had first told Lord Bute of the haunting of B—— was among these.

An interesting light on the effect of prayer would probably be brought out by struggles against witchcraft, struggles doubtless very common amongst early Christians. Indeed, the devils who were cast out must sometimes have been baffled hypnotists confronted by One who was stronger than they; the departing into the swine is much more intelligible on this hypothesis than on Dean Farrar's, of the swine's terror, which suppresses the "devils'" request.

A story is told of Titus by the rabbis: he heard a gnawing sound at his brain;

it caused him great pain.   He heard a
blacksmith hammering at his anvil, and
the gnawing ceased.   The blacksmith was
paid to go on hammering in Titus' neighbourhood.   At the end of a few days the
"animal" that gnawed at his brain got
indifferent to the hammering, went on
gnawing, and Titus died.   His brain was
opened, and an animal as big as a spar-
row with a beak of iron was found in it.
The truth of this story would be, that
some magicians, not especially adroit hypnotists, hammered at Titus' tympanum.
His nerves, tried by climatic fever—a
great facilitator of hypnotism — and by
debauchery, gave way, and Jerusalem was
avenged.

The writer once approached a very
eminent Catholic cleric on the subject,
hoping that some Freemason who had
been victimised by tricks played by
hypnotists in Italy might have relieved

his conscience to the priests; the writer had been given one clue in the following way.

Two English Freemasons in the writer's presence had briefly mentioned mesmerism in Italian lodges. One asking a question as to this being true, the other, who objected to his son becoming a Freemason early, turned the question off; it is possible that he suspected it was the case, but preferred holding his tongue.

Now as these scoundrel hypnotists have, unseen but heard, approached three or four people to the writer's knowledge, under the pretence of being connected with Freemasonry, it is very possible that they may have induced some of their victims to enter a lodge, and then or before tricked them in different ways. Indeed, one of the people attacked unsuccessfully had, to the writer's knowledge, an absurd idea of the exclusiveness of

Freemasonry, since he objected to the Prince of Wales making over a poor Freemason's brief (if that be the proper word to use) for inquiry as to his circumstances to gentlemen who were not Freemasons. The brief of course contained only the man's name, and a few ornamental figures : the man was dead and his widow wanted help. It is to be wished that some scientific Freemason would study the matter ; he would see that the secrecy of Freemasonry, however harmless and venial, affords cover for blackguard hypnotists of this particular and doubtless rare kind. This secrecy is of course entirely conventional, and could doubtless be altered. As elsewhere, the people who take an interest in it are not always people with broad and scientific minds, and at the close of the eighteenth century Cagliostro misused it, it is said, for his own purposes.

The writer regrets that a want of scientific study of the subject (it must be remembered that books on hypnotism were rare, and research backward eleven years ago) prevented him from introducing the subject properly to the wise and good Lord Carnarvon. It must be borne in mind that for audible thought-transfers to lead not only to apparent intercourse — the answers being put into the recipient's mouth, as in Mrs. Godfrey's case—a pretence of something like Freemasonry is needed.

In "Piccadilly" Oliphant describes a cross appearing to the hero, and the words "live the life" being whispered to him. He then abandons the young woman he loves to his friend. Such a course of conduct would certainly be suggested by hypnotists to make a capable man their plaything and tool as was the case with Oliphant. Obviously a man could live a more beneficial life with a marriage of mutual affection, whilst a poor young woman would, if she married otherwise, be sure to be a sufferer. Perhaps this fragment was historical. It would have made the Oliphants' disaster easier.

A word, a vision, and the mischief is done. Perhaps poor Captain Lestrange was forced into his unhappy marriage by a similar trick.

The love of power and of bullying is so great, perhaps especially with British and Germans, that this tyranny is not wonderful; were there not an efficient police the Mohawks would soon revive; the infamous cruelty of some brutes is only known to a few doctors. Envy, malice, hatred, and all uncharitableness are shown in these attacks upon people, whose lives were useful and whose characters were high. Possibly the hope of profit may be sometimes present;—when

this is past and the scoundrels have had
their triumph, their persecution is con-
tinued, unprofitable though it be; partly
to render pursuit more difficult, partly
maybe for practice, partly because they
have acquired a horrible habit which they
cannot get rid of. Du Potet's feeling of
pride becomes in the bosom of a blackguard wholly evil. Much interest has
been given to Home's feats: to his float-
ing outside his window and other extra-
ordinary performances. His first feat, be
it remembered, was to make a rapping
stool leap up when it had a Bible on it,
and leap all the harder. Was not this mere
tricking action on the observer's eye and
ear? This was closely paralleled by the
rascals about B——, who made a "work-
table, a box on long slender legs," emit a
loud bang. Home might have done this
alone to his aunt, but it possibly was done
by a combination of people at B——.

The fact that Home, at least on one occasion, could not do anything when Houdin was near, seems to show that Home relied on an accomplice whom he was unable to conceal from Houdin, and who doubtless was a hypnotist also.

It is a fortunate thing that "spiritualism" and its wonders have invited scientific study. The tendency to become spiritists is, of course, furthered in many by an uncomfortable belief that without spiritualism a future life is not insured; only the coming again to them of the spirits of the dead assures them that they rise again.

Of course all the heathen ideas of a resurrection were founded on the keen recollection of themselves the defunct have inspired. Our belief in the Christian revelations is founded on its ethical system, part of which, however, is of course for missionary effort only, but

which is the more remarkably connected
with previous revelations, not so distinctly
reported, to the Jews, and with the history
of the world at large.

Of course spiritual impressions are of
no more value than the stigmata on
hysterical girls, in whom the emotional
element was over developed, and the
religious understanding too little developed.   The reversion to ancestor worship
in spiritism seems more clear, and dinners
at Kensal Green with five shillings tomb
money, after the system of some low-
caste Indian tribes, should be instituted
by the spiritists.   But the Chinaman also
conciliates other spirits—those of friends
or patrons or the great men of past
generations; why do not the spiritualists
sacrifice gold leaf and roast pork like
the inhabitants of the Far East?

The Catholic Church has exorcised
spirits and put them in their place as

E

improper and disturbing elements. It thereby told its members that spirits were conjurable : of course really the minds of the members were strengthened, but the toleration of the idea of spirits, whether lazy and trifling, pernicious or beneficial, is of course wrong. However, as they were considered the servants of sorcerers, the idea was in some respects sufficiently accurate.

The Lutheran Church in Denmark, in the last century, had many famous exorcisers who banned ghosts into Schleswig-Holstein.

One hypnotiser against another, the battle-field a stupid peasant. M. Flammarion's book, just published (July 1900), contains an instance or two of French peasants bewitching one another. The cure for this witchcraft is found in science, the criminal law, and the mutual kindness that, derived from Christianity, though

often promoted by men whom we can
only call God-fearing unbelievers, has
grown so much in this century, and
more elsewhere even than in Britain.
Thousands of poor people perished in
the days of old, guiltless victims, whilst
some scoundrelly hypnotists went free.
In modern times some poor people,
bothered by hypnotists, have been sent
to lunatic asylums and have fallen victims
of the greed, cruelty, and neglect that so
often prevail there.   One must give Dr.
Savage his due, that he describes a case
in his book on insanity where a lady hearing voices (cheating hypnotic voices,
perhaps), and believing herself insulted,
left one lodging after another perfectly
quietly, and he admits that this case was
not suitable for a lunatic asylum.

The " spirits " of spiritists are, of course,
not impressive, if their somewhat startling
amount of information be excepted.   The

language used by George Pelham is pure twaddle. One member of the society seems to have been hypnotised, and the rest studied by the Piper gang through him.

If all a man feels, sees, and hears be noted, the information gathered, coming from a stranger, will be startling to people who belong to his circle of friends.

This information was imparted to Mrs. Piper, where it had not been collected by her. All she saw was seen by her accomplices, who advised her accordingly. They were doubtless too busy to study the eminent statesman whom she told that he had money transactions with a person called George.[1]

Study and inquiry should eradicate the superstition and the fraud called spiritism, and people should be protected against a most dangerous and cowardly form of

[1] Miss Goodrich Freer's "Essays," p. 119.

crime—criminal hypnotism.   It enfeebles
the mind; and murder is hardly more
serious to a man than a marriage that
embitters his life, or the loss of a career
that is the moral stay of his existence.
The knowledge that such a thing exists
would, if it induced one per cent. more
care, save many lives.   Apparitions of
beneficent spirits can be easily accounted
for.   They are cases of automatic visuali-
sation.   Thus the children mentioned in
the late Mr. Spurgeon's Life, who went
down an underground passage and saw a
vision of their dead mother, who stopped
them from falling into a well, felt as
other children would feel, that they must
think of the one person who is always
ready to preserve her little children from
terror and pain; and thinking of her,
they visualised her.

Energy and intelligence are the worst
enemies of criminal hypnotism, as they

are of burglary, but social organisation alone can combat crime.

To note some particulars of the haunting of B—— besides those already mentioned. The butler, Sanders, lived with the H. family at B—— the year before Miss Freer garrisoned the house. Not one of the people who were at B—— in 1896 were there with Miss Freer. This bars one type of fraud being alleged. Sanders, besides hearing thumping, groans, and the rustling of a lady's dress, had his bedclothes lifted up and let fall again—"first at the foot of my bed, but gradually coming towards the head." He held the clothes round his neck with his hands, but they were "gently lifted in spite of my efforts to hold them."

This simply means that he had cramps, resulting from the effect of hypnotism on the muscles of his legs. The writer

believes that the force always acts from
the feet, or rather one foot, upwards;
obviously a man sitting or standing up
must be approached that way, and habit
causes the electric stream to flow in that
direction.   But this cramp is not felt so
keenly as is the case when cramp arises
from a constrained position.   The conse-
quence is that the kicks given to relieve
it are not so violent and decisive.   They
are repeated automatically, until the bed-
clothes fly up finally near the head, as
is described.   The intervals between the
flights of the clothes seem shorter than
they are; this is again due to hypnotic
influence, as in spiritistic performances
and in conjuring, where, as M. Binet
has recently remarked, a little hypnotism
always comes in.

Thus in Mr. Austin Podmore's account
of Mr. Davey's séance, his attention was
called away for two or three minutes with-

out his noting it. We may take it for granted that the kickings up of the bed-clothes during which Sanders became weak and faint, lasted ten minutes or more. "Being fanned as though some bird were flying round my head," arose from his own breath after his efforts; he felt it the more as he had got warm.[1] The sound of breathing may have been of his own, but is not unlikely to have been the transferred sound of the breathing of one of two people hypnotising him. The feeling of the bed being carried round (or moved) towards the window is a feeling of reaction: a man sticks his back against the bed to resist the material and mental pressure, and the relief felt as the effort ceases gives him the impression that the bed has been swung towards the window, towards which he naturally looks, since the slight draught refreshes

[1] "Alleged Haunting," p. 46.

him and diverts the attack. That he actually felt some one making passes over him is not an error; he had two antagonists; one of whom, like the young engineer Cleave,[1] was hypnotised by the other, both willing the hypnotism of Sanders.

He felt the passes the stronger antagonist was making over the other. If one of the two people can obtain return messages like Mr. Godfrey, intimate knowledge of his victim's doings might soon be obtained. A ghost appeared to young H. in the shape of a veiled lady; perhaps the mist round her was taken for a veil. But to return to the action of two hypnotists on one person, it may be noted that the sound like the giving of a tin box heard by Miss Moore, Miss Freer, and Miss Langton,[2]

---

[1] "Osgood Mason," p. 234.
[2] "Haunting of B—— House," p. 155.

and afterwards like the lid of a coal-scuttle caught by a dress by Mrs. M.,[1] was the sound of a gong doubtless used to stimulate the hypnotised partner in the blackguard couple. Such a sound done with a little spring gong, or with a larger one, has been heard by a victim.

By such experience, too, the monotonous reading can be explained; it was the commencement by less powerful hypnotists of a supporting attack: the words would become audible, distinguishable, and noticeable later. This might ensue after the victim was more deeply hypnotised.

Probably the very words which were to be used later were used then, a sort of sub-conscious memory being created.

Apparitions of a misty nature are described by Podmore in his chapter on " Haunted Houses."[2] Miss Langton saw

---

[1] " Haunting of B—— House," p. 173.
[2] " Studies," pp. 315, 326.

a misty phantom, and Lizzie the housemaid saw a cloud and afterwards got a
cramp, less persistent than the butler's,
as she began to scream.[1]   The upper
housemaid saw a woman whose legs she
did not notice,[2] as was the case with
Mr. Godfrey's friend to whom he appeared hypnotically.

The fact that the dog that appeared to
Miss Freer was a spaniel like Major S.'s,
shows familiarity with the house on the
part of the gang.

That they moved about early near the
house is shown by Mr. C. hearing the
caw of the rooks at 5.35 on March 6;
they would not start cawing so early
unless disturbed.   There is thus abundant
evidence (1) that rascals were at work;
(2) accounting for certain of the phenomena observed; (3) pointing out their

---

[1] "Haunting of B—— House," p. 167.
[2] *Ibid.*, pp. 205, 207.

resemblance to cases of experimental hallucinations or thought transfer ; (4) that such hypnotic operations could be traced by due vigilance. No. 2 is based in part on the writer's experience.

If the roads and neighbourhood had been patrolled, and exposure to possible hypnotists avoided, the phenomena would have ceased. The gentleman who wrote to the *Times* made a point or two that were too petty to notice, and was probably disagreeable to Miss Freer, but detective work would have been useful. The gentleman's connection with a class of men, the mad doctors whom the late Sir William Gull so rightly despised, and whose observations have been so unscientific, may perhaps have unduly prejudiced Miss Freer against him. Yet people have listened to a Maudsley against an Esher, and gone to the other extreme. Perhaps Miss Freer will reconsider her opinion, that hypnotism is for doctors only to study.

To wind up with a statement of what the writer believes to have been the object of the rascals about B——; ordinary thought-transfer probably precedes audible speech by hypnotic influence.

The many people who hear their names called, and find that no death or other striking occurrence coincides in time with this, are perhaps being experimented on by hypnotists, who somehow or other, perhaps by community of feeling, have hit upon the precise moment of a state of subconscious expectation that makes transfer of an actual word easier.

Of course people, friends or others, about the victim are an antidote to influences. The inevitable tendency of pious natures, sensitive people who are indispensable to society, is to self-blame. In misfortune they would always blame themselves as sinners who deserved punishment, probably from having paid previously an undeserved attention to the censorious. Their frame of mind is very contrary to the gospel teaching, and to science ; but the division of labour is moral as well as material ; one man takes the kicks undeservedly, another the halfpence undeservedly. These gentle people can thus be driven into apparently insane acts, if they have fools about them.

The fact of the name Ishbel being transferred to the inquirers assembled at Ballechin, may indicate whose was the spirit that should profess to preach to victims. Women are often said to be worse, if evil, than men, and they play this ugly rôle better.

That rain interrupted the phenomena is another point against the partisans of the supernatural. When after rain the nun was surprised and chased by Miss

Freer, it would seem that she intended mischief to some other member of the garrison at B——, or she would have been *en rapport* with Miss Freer, and aware that she was nearing her.

The pronunciation of the names Ishbel and Margaret only indicate a non-Highlander being implicated, but it seems possible that the latter name, for which there was no particular cause, may have been a punning appellation. Mar—garret, as the grey woman, attacked the servants in the attics. Such a joke is characteristic of such villains, and shows that they are tolerably educated people. Their avoiding Mr. Z. may indicate that they may have been brought in contact with him, in the fifty different ways that an editor may have seen people—their contributing to the press is not impossible. They must have some money too. The writer believes that physiology and many other branches of science, notably social, will be benefited by studying this case.

Lord Bute, Miss Freer, Colonel Taylor, and other members of the "garrison," deserve the gratitude of society. May inquirers never rest until the subject, not too difficult a one in the age of electricians and physiologists, has been fairly cleared up.

There are one or two points in the study of the advanced combined hypnotism—it is probably always criminal—which are worthy of notice. One is that the operators generally, or always—(observation is difficult)—repeat a phrase or its most important words. The first saying of the word is barely noticeable. The repetition forces the word to the subject's attention.

Secondly, speech is addressed to the right ear; the sufferer of course declines attention to it, but this slight, almost automatic effort, yet distracts attention from the left ear, and a communication to that ear is unheard, but perceived as a thought.

To detect speech a very trifling pressure on the ear has to be watched for. In a law court or in society the interest of what is going on knocks the operators out.

A facility for receiving thought transferred makes a person perhaps more susceptible to depression by dull or inferior people, but principle partly cures this.

The art of dismissing obtrusive thoughts and persisting in one's own has to be cultivated by people with the readiest perceptions.

Natural caution and a habit of studying probabilities are great helps against such attackers ; but, on the other hand, the man who drinks a glass of wine when he

F

feels low will beat the hypnotist, who will doubtless harm him by causing degeneration.

A glass of port wine at eleven in the morning, and tea or breakfast early, are a great help. Early rising deprives the operators of the time when they pin their victim best.

A dog's bark, a peahen's cry, above all a bird's song, is a great interruption to hypnotism—silent or by voices. A nightingale will foil the worst attack.

The scoundrels may try and substitute an ugly sound for the song of birds; they cannot affect the sharp, short, and sudden cry of the swallow.

Walking up and down hill is much better than walking on the flat. The air is forced harder through the lungs. Windy weather is a help, and rain, for two reasons: it is an advantage to the victim, and keeps rascals away. The writer believes that the cartilages are influenced, or at least felt to be influenced, rather than the nerves, glands, or even the muscles.

He believes that the hearing of the voices of hypnotists is partly brought about by a change in the cartilages of the ear, which (it is stated in Grey's anatomy) are to a certain extent disintegrated by electricity.

The ears thus become rather telephonic, and no longer dependent so entirely on the will; emotion, however, either checks this facility of sound or the weakness that permits attention.

If to this be added the repetition by various voices of the same word, the first occasion probably when the subject's eye is seen to pass over the printed passage where it occurs in a paper, words will be brought to the victim's ear hypnotically.

But perhaps the first system mentioned

is used where the difficulties of approach are greater, the rascals must have great patience.

When the victim begins a letter the date is called to him, and then he can be tested by calling, say, July to him in September. His name may be called when in reverie, perhaps in the country, his mind goes back to his boyhood.

Thought reading is very easy if a person is visible, and rascals begin from a distance, and finally operate between hypnotics out of sight.

They seem in this first to catch a person when he passes a window. This shows that they are susceptible to the amount of light, as well as that a thick wall is a greater obstacle than a pane of glass. They thus too may partly distinguish environment, though this is perhaps learned by practice.

Ear and eye and muscular feeling are

all weighed. A strong man much hypnotised in this way, will notice that a
diminished light will relieve him, although previously he paid little attention
to any glare, even up to the age of forty.

Residence changed from a ground floor
to a lofty room would often cause unusual
relief. On a church tower this would be
felt even more.

The noise of London, and the fact that
people hanging about are watched, are
checks to the early operations of criminal
hypnotists.

Music is probably an excellent antidote.
A feeling of stupidity, given even for a
second, would probably give a boy a wrong
idea of himself, and even repeated suc-
cesses would not quite efface this.

The Japanese system of wrestling lately
introduced shows how powerful a touch
on a nerve may be in weakening a man.
Such a touch transferred or propelled,

may for a long time aid hypnotisers from a distance, though it would be in time disregarded or little regarded.

Calculative work is better suited than imaginative work to free the brain. I would urge inquirers to ask themselves, whether Mrs. Piper's doings could be accounted for in any other way than that suggested.

Clairvoyance is seemingly mere guess-work, the imagination being heightened temporarily rather than depressed by the hypnotic pressure. Mr. Vincent's analysis of mental reactions is invaluable. A hypnotised person does not go on to the analogies, which may be quite obvious from a suggestive word.

This resembles the habit of some religious persons who build on one text of the Bible, completely neglecting the modifying and explanatory text that immediately follows. The subject is grossly credulous, and is deprived of much fruitful time for thinking.

The hypnotised person will refuse to do many actions, and religion is of course a mainstay, though irrational accretions, fasting, and superstitious views of the Communion will weaken it.

Miss Freer repeatedly asked herself the question, "How did this come into my head?"

It would seem from the story of the red figure, afterwards recognised on a seal, that she had been hypnotised not by her companion but by some travelling rascal who had seen the letter in the post-office, and thus brought off a piece of prevision.

Intelligent watchfulness is a great protection.

Printed by BALLANTYNE, HANSON & Co.
Edinburgh & London

Published by Philip Wellby

6 *Henrietta Street, Covent Garden, W.C.*

Psychic Philosophy

As the Foundation of a Religion of
Natural Law

By V. C. DESERTIS

WITH INTRODUCTORY NOTE BY

ALFRED RUSSEL WALLACE,

D.C.L., LL.D., F.R.S.

New Edition. 3s. 6d. net.

Notes on the Margins

Being Suggestions of Thought and Enquiry

FIVE ESSAYS BY

CLIFFORD HARRISON

1. AN ENQUIRY INTO MYSTICISM.
2. THE ILLUSION OF REALISM.
3. THE LINES OF COINCIDENCE.
4. ARREST OR ADVANCE?
5. THE LOST RICHES OF THE WORLD.

Cheaper Issue. 3s. 6d.

The Hidden Way Across the Threshold

By J. C. STREET

12s. net.

The Sound of a Voice that is Still

By ARCHIE CAMPBELL

3s. 6d.

The Life of Louis Claude de Saint-Martin

The Unknown Philosopher, and the Substance of His Transcendental Doctrine

By ARTHUR EDWARD WAITE

10s. net.

Lightning Source UK Ltd.
Milton Keynes UK
UKHW020011100223
416721UK00002B/555